The Astrology Book

The Astrology Book copyright ©1995 by Armand Eisen. All rights reserved. Printed in Singapore. No part of this book may be used or reproduced in any manner whatsoever without written permission except in the case of reprints in the context of reviews. For information write Andrews and McMeel, a Universal Press Syndicate Company, 4900 Main Street, Kansas City, Missouri 64112.

Frontispiece: Robyn Officer

The text of this book was set in Opti-Cuba Libre and Adobe Duc De Berry by Junie Lee

Book design by Junie Lee

ISBN: 0-8362-4742-6

The Astrology Book

by Julia Bondi

Ariel Books
Andrews and McMeel
Kansas City

Introduction

The twelve constellations (the groups of stars that make up the twelve signs of the zodiac) form a ring in the sky through which the sun appears to travel during the course of the year. Whichever starry region the sun occupied on the date of your birth determines your sun sign, the astrological sign that has the greatest influence on character, personality, and potential.

For instance, if you were born between February 20 and March 20, the sun was tracking through the stars of *Pisces*, thus *Pisces* is your sun sign. Whether or not you "believe in the stars," you'll be amazed to discover how many personality traits you share with others born under your same sign. Look up the sun signs of your friends: you're sure to find the same uncanny likenesses.

Will a *Libra* and a *Taurus* get along? Which signs are meant for each other? Which ones are in for trouble? You'll find the answers in the compatibility guide following each sun sign. Astrology may not be an exact science, but it's a fascinating one and it's fun.

Aries

(MARCH 21 – APRIL 20)

Aries the Ram is the first sign of the heavenly zodiac. Ariens are always motivated by the desire to know themselves and to be the best they can be. Independence, courage, self-esteem, and enthusiasm come naturally to them. Their passion for life is unbounded, especially when it concerns what is most dear to them—their families, friends, ideals, and goals. They work hard and are often pioneers and innovators in their chosen fields. Rams are impulsive; they can also be rude and selfish when they are thwarted in pursuing their goals. A supportive mate can help them to realize all of their dreams and become the leaders they yearn to be.

Aries &...

Aries: A dynamic duo whose passions will bring them together but will provide little balance as they face the struggles of life.

Taurus: Aries needs the stability that sensual, affectionate Taurus can give, and Taurus will benefit from the inspiration provided by Aries.

Gemini: These two will never bore each other and will make wonderful companions. Trusting each other is of the utmost importance for this match to last.

Cancer: Cancer's nurturing and loyal nature will attract Aries, but the Crab may be frustrated by the Ram's excessive independence.

Leo: Aries encourages; Leo supports and guides. This happy duo will enjoy a loving and lasting partnership.

Virgo: These signs are too different to mesh. Aries will disrupt Virgo's orderly existence, and Virgo's criticisms will drive Aries away.

Libra: A toss-up. Either true harmony or constant tension will rule this relationship as Libra tries to soothe Aries' restlessness and Aries attempts to lure Libra into a fuller life.

Scorpio: A sensual and dramatic pairing. A few problems may arise if Aries is put off by Scorpio's sarcasm, or if Scorpio balks at following Aries' lead.

Sagittarius: Both want to lead the way: who will follow? A common goal will be necessary for these two to balance and support each other.

Capricorn: Together these two can conquer anything. Changing old habits is the secret to the success of this match, which means listening to each other and learning to cooperate.

Aquarius: Common goals and shared ideals make this a powerful combination between two complex and strong-willed signs.

Pisces: Attraction and repulsion will define this relationship because these two are a mystery to each other. Misunderstandings will be common but can be overcome.

Taurus

(APRIL 21 – MAY 21)

Taurus the Bull is a comfortable inhabitant of the earth: sensual, affectionate, cautious, loving, and loyal. Happiness for the Bull is having someone to love and something to do. Taureans demand to be appreciated, however, and they insist on absolute fidelity. Taureans are practical; they work hard at building relationships and secure, stable environments. The results of their labors are success and contentment. Bulls are infinitely patient; they are also obstinate, with a tendency to sulk, and if pushed too far, inclined to fly into rages. Never demand of a Bull: you will only arouse ire. Ask, however, and the Bull will happily comply.

Taurus &...

Aries: Taurus will find Aries too pushy and demanding for lasting comfort. Intimacy will be difficult for these two.

Taurus: A natural affinity exits between two good-natured, affectionate Bulls. However, hard work will be needed to keep this relationship from going stale.

Gemini: This is a common but difficult combination. Taurus enjoys Gemini's charm and wit but the Twins' flightiness may not sit right with the earthbound Bull.

Cancer: Love and security are possible here but the Crab's fabled moods and the Bull's famous sulks may challenge the stability of this relationship.

Leo: These two are stubborn and easily offended, but they adore each other. A high degree of flexibility and sensitivity is essential for this match to last.

Virgo: This can be a wonderful union. Taurus may feel let down, however, if Virgo isn't forthcoming with all the little indulgences the Bull desires.

Libra: If Libra remains physically demonstrative, and Taurus doesn't become too controlling, a rich, successful, and lasting union is possible.

Scorpio: The ultimate match. These two are true soul mates who will share deep feelings, profound intimacy, and a lasting affection.

Sagittarius: This odd combination can be a harmonious one. Sound wisdom from the Bull and bold truth telling from the Archer make it work.

Capricorn: A great and satisfying love is possible between Taurus and Capricorn if they always treat each other with respect.

Aquarius: Friendship should be the goal with these two: intimacy will be difficult. Aquarius's need for independence will make the Bull feel shut out and resentful.

Pisces: The romantic ideal is possible between dreamy Pisces and protective Taurus. As long as Pisces is loyal, this relationship will thrive.

Gemini

(MAY 22–JUNE 21)

Gemini is the sign of the Twins, whose fabled diversity is the essence of Gemini's charm, wit, and brilliance. Geminis adore words, ideas, opportunities, and people. The Twins are the ultimate communicators, here to tell us a story, tweak our curiosity, and lead us to new discoveries. Only if Geminis live life fully, visit enough places, meet enough people, exhaust enough possibilities, and pursue enough ideas, will they be satisfied. They are driven to excel. So long as their personal independence isn't challenged, they can be very involved, loyal, and delightful. They cherish their friends, relatives, and children, and they can truly love if they are loved in return, and encouraged to develop their myriad selves.

Gemini &...

Aries: A lasting attraction and smooth-running relationship is possible here. Aries can provide the motivation; Gemini the direction.

Taurus: Though Gemini appreciates the love Taurus offers, complying with the demands of the earthbound and home-oriented Bull will be difficult for the social and independent Twins.

Gemini: Numerous shared interests will make for a great beginning—but that's it. Friendship will be much easier for these twin signs.

Cancer: Affection and respect are possible here, but Cancer's emotional twists and turns may prove too overwhelming for the lighthearted Twins.

Leo: Gemini will thrive on the Lion's solicitude and will be attentive in return—at least until Leo's need for constant attention threatens the Twins' autonomy.

Virgo: For Gemini and Virgo to sustain their interest and meet each other's needs, they have only to try—and they will succeed.

Libra: A harmonious pair who enjoy each other and a lively social life. Dedication to home and family will make a strong bond between these two.

Scorpio: A volatile, exciting, and passionate duo, but one destined for trouble. The gregarious and popular Gemini may never be able to satisfy Scorpio's excessive requirements for commitment.

Sagittarius: Two fascinating signs who will find each other stimulating company and good traveling companions. But who will keep the home fires burning?

Capricorn: No luck here for Gemini. The Twins envy Capricorn's perseverance and success, but can't abide the Goat's bossy nature.

Aquarius: A good, solid relationship is genuinely possible here. Aquarius will bring some stability to Gemini's life, and Gemini will be curious to learn what makes Aquarius tick.

Pisces: The deep emotional realms in which Pisces is comfortable may be cause for panic with the Twins.

Cancer

(June 22–July 23)

Cancer is the sign of the Crab, an image that illustrates the true Cancerian nature. On the surface is a cool, calm, nurturing, competent, and kind person. Beneath that protective shell, however, is a vulnerable, sensitive, cautious, and sometimes fearful person. Cancer is both the little child seeking security and love and the capable adult nurturing family and community. Cancers are imaginative, moody, and intuitive. They are also exceedingly empathetic, which allows them to tune in easily to their emotional environment. Their equally sharp business sense is also a valuable asset. Cancers need a quiet, harmonious home where they can recharge their batteries and soothe their jangled nerves. Love, security, and a sense of connection through family, friends, and work are imperative for the Cancer to enjoy life to the fullest.

Cancer &...

Aries: This is a difficult combination. Cancer's moods upset Aries, who is also changeable, but doesn't know it.

Taurus: Cancer admires Taurean values and integrity and is a natural to nurture and sustain the Bull. Both desire a family and a secure future. This is a strong bond.

Gemini: Gemini's whimsical nature appeals to Cancer, but the Crab can't really understand the Twins' world and, in the long run, won't feel comfortable in it.

Cancer: This pairing of like signs will probably spark more drama and sensitivity than either party can tolerate. Cancer needs a calmer, more grounded partner.

Leo: Cancer adores the drama and generosity of the leonine personality and is drawn to Leo's radiant confidence. The Crab won't mind stroking the Lion's enormous ego—as long as security is the reward.

Virgo: This is a natural and common partnership between two signs who desire the basics: home, family, success, and security.

Libra: If Libra is not too detached and Cancer not too preoccupied with emotional traumas, this match has great potential for longevity.

Scorpio: Despite their profoundly sensitive natures, these two would be better off as friends than lovers. Cancer's moodiness and Scorpio's sarcasm may set them against each other.

Sagittarius: An exciting attraction. Both these signs enjoy giving and getting a great deal of attention.

Capricorn: These opposites are so devoted to family, home, and security that a match seems inevitable. Cancer coddles and nurtures Capricorn; Capricorn guides and supports Cancer.

Aquarius: Surprisingly, Aquarius and Cancer are drawn to each other. Cancer is all feelings; Aquarius is all ideas. Both, however, are so changeable that they implicitly understand each other.

Pisces: These two would seem to make an ideal pair emotionally, but they don't. They can lose themselves in their inner worlds of feeling and forget to be available to each other.

Leo

(JULY 24–AUGUST 23)

Leos, symbolized by the proud Lion, possessor of the ultimate heart of hearts, are charismatic, creative, and joyful individuals who love themselves, life, and everyone and everything in it. They enjoy life to the utmost. Leos are capable and desirous of romance, fidelity, and trust, the grand gesture, and the exalted destiny. They bubble with such a zest for life that they need only to find worthy outlets for their energies to be utterly happy. A consuming passion, an adored family, loyal friends, and/or rewarding work will all suffice. Leos love to share their pleasures, but they need to be loved and appreciated in return, because it is only by receiving love and admiration that they come to trust fully their own abilities. They are nurtured by praise and respect, and self-esteem is the foundation of their being. To attack or insult the dignity of a Leo is to break the Lion's heart—and risk the Lion's roar.

Leo &...

Aries: These two can enjoy each other's company without undue complications. Aries and Leo both want to live life fully, so they will focus on living and go forward together.

Taurus: Leo adores the affectionate Taurus, and gives so much to the Bull that it is easy for them to be happy together. This match has great romantic potential.

Gemini: These two are a natural. The Lion and the Twins make a wonderful audience for each other and can have wonderful times together.

Cancer: This affectionate match may occasionally turn into a childish sulk: Cancer can behave like a needy baby and Leo like a dramatic child. Who will play the adult?

Leo: Two stars cannot occupy the same stage. Leos need constant ego stroking and someone to care for. These two should look beyond the mirror for a partner.

Virgo: Leos like to spoil their partners, which will be difficult for Virgos to accept. And Leo's ego will be easily and constantly bruised by the Virgin's critical nature.

Libra: The potential is here for a great romance since Libra and Leo are both in love with love. The Lion gets great satisfaction from showing off its lovely Libran prize.

Scorpio: A surprisingly passionate combination that will create sparks of excitement and tension. Once these two commit to each other, they will stick it out through thick and thin.

Sagittarius: Affection and spontaneity will keep these two fun-loving signs together as long as Sagittarius is never stifled, and Leo never insulted or betrayed.

Capricorn: Royal battles are likely here. Leo respects the Goat's drive and loyalty but cannot bow down to Capricorn's authority.

Aquarius: A difficult match. Aquarius's independent nature will cause Leo to feel unneeded. And Aquarius's wide circle of friends will rouse the Lion's jealousy.

Pisces: A love match. Pisces will be devoted to Leo and enjoy being cradled in the Lion's love. This union will result in creative expression, mutual support, and deep satisfaction.

Virgo
(AUGUST 24–SEPTEMBER 23)

This is the sign of the Virgin holding sheaves of wheat, an image that captures the true definition of Virgos: gentle, honest, capable people with pure intentions, a quiet sensuality, and a calm attachment to the natural world. Virgos see the essence of life as hard work and patient effort; they strive to be conscious in their thoughts, truthful and accurate in their words, responsible and competent in their work, kind and helpful to their loved ones, and humble and worthy in their life. Through all this effort they will achieve a great deal, but they may ask too little in return. Virgos know instinctively how to work and serve, but they must learn to express their need for appreciation. Their celebrated fussiness and criticism is partly an attempt to be noticed, and partly an attempt to be helpful—they never criticize out of spite or meanness. An orderly, calm existence is essential to their security and happiness.

Virgo &...

Aries: Virgo will not settle easily into the tumultuous rhythm of life with Aries. The virgin's helpful nature will be appreciated but the orderly existence so necessary to Virgo will be impossible for the Ram.

Taurus: Virgo and Taurus both seek a calm and stable life. If Virgo is demonstrative to the affectionate Bull, this union can have real staying power.

Gemini: Virgo is impressed by Gemini's natural ease. However, for this twosome to flourish, the Virgin will have to become much more social and willing to forego a certain amount of domesticity.

Cancer: Cancer desires a deep and genuine intimacy. If Virgo can fulfill this desire, a happy and serene life is possible for these steadfast and sympathetic signs.

Leo: Leo's generosity and dignity appeal to the Virgin, and Virgo's devotion appeals to the Lion. However, the Virgin's critical nature may mar this union.

Virgo: A lack of passion and excitement in this same-sign pairing may lead to stagnation and a host of missed opportunities.

Libra: Virgo likes to simplify and save; Libra likes to expand and spend. A struggle for balance may be necessary here but the potential for happiness is great.

Scorpio: Scorpio's intensity thrills and intimidates the Virgin who can provide the serenity that Scorpio seeks. Life together for these two can be very therapeutic, satisfying, and challenging.

Sagittarius: Virgo has knowledge; Sagittarius has wisdom. Their life choices, however, are far too different to work: Virgo wants a home; Sagittarius wants the world.

Capricorn: These two hardworking signs can appreciate and complement each other. Virgo needs a loved one to work with and for, and Capricorn needs to lead and be respected.

Aquarius: Not a promising pairing. Virgo will feel perpetually insecure living with the distant affections of Aquarius who cannot be bothered to provide the constant reassurances the Virgin needs to feel loved.

Pisces: Virgo can be a loving support and guide to dreamy Pisces. In return, Pisces will either shower the Virgin with love and compassion or be frustratingly impenetrable and withdrawn. Virgo takes a risk here.

Libra

(SEPTEMBER 24–OCTOBER 23)

Libra is the sign of the Scales, which symbolize justice, equality, harmony, and beauty. Libras seek balance in equal and harmonious relationships. The Scales are the sign of marriage and partnership and it is through the other that Libra finds fulfillment. Libras are the beautiful people—graceful, stylish, and charming: their partners are special, their friends plentiful, their children gifted. Libras are often artists, and they frequently find themselves surrounded by creative, successful, and talented colleagues and friends. Social grace, popularity, and diplomacy are Libran qualities, and though they are subject to indecisiveness, it is most often visible when they sense disapproval from those they love. Considering the opinions and feelings of others is Libra's way of creating harmony. If others are happy, Libra is too.

Libra &...

Aries: If Aries will only be nice, Libra will find the Ram's company stimulating and desirable. And Aries will be calmed and soothed by Libra's gentle nature.

Taurus: Taurus can be the perfect balance for Libra's lavish style of life, and the Bull will feel flattered and secure in partnership with the Scales.

Gemini: This is the social partner Libra craves, whose wit and charm complement Libra's talents. However, commitment will always be an issue with this pairing.

Cancer: Cancer offers solace, comfort, love, and security. Libra, however, will soon feel under siege by the Crab's emotional swings.

Leo: Love and romance will thrive in this happy union between the lovers of the zodiac. But both must come down to earth to make this relationship last.

Virgo: The Virgin may be a little dull for Libra, and decidedly too critical. Both appreciate beauty and truth, and can share much as friends—as lovers, boredom and resentment are too likely.

Libra: Two Libras can easily fall in love—but who will mind the store? If they can solve that question, there might be hope for this duo.

Scorpio: Libra sees a challenge in the conquest of Scorpio. Eventually, however, the mild-mannered Scales may not be comfortable with Scorpio's fierce intensity.

Sagittarius: Libra prefers the status quo; Sagittarius likes to rock the boat, which, sooner or later, will make this a rocky relationship.

Capricorn: Together, these two ambitious and goal-oriented signs can climb any mountain. The Goat can give Libra many things—starting with commitment.

Aquarius: This combination has genuine staying power. These two can enjoy life and romance without exerting too much pressure on each other.

Pisces: Pisces is too otherworldly, distracted, and self-absorbed to be a satisfying partner for Libra who, in turn, is too social and self-indulgent to suit Pisces.

Scorpio

(OCTOBER 24–NOVEMBER 23)

Scorpio is the sign of the Scorpion. It is the challenge of Scorpios to rise above their own tendency toward extremes and to soar to the heights of success. Scorpios are often faced with the decision whether to take the high road or the low. They are intense, perceptive, determined, passionate, jealous, and revengeful. It is important for them to marry, and to work with and to choose as friends those who are as trustworthy as they are. However, be aware that you will never totally know Scorpios because part of their nature is reserved for them alone and cannot be shared with anyone. They will give themselves as completely as they can to those they love and trust, and because they have so much to give, this may prove more than enough.

$\mathcal{S}corpio$ &...

Aries: A passionate pairing between two very powerful signs who can share adventure and glory. Fighting for control and differences of opinion may make this a combative match, however.

Taurus: These two sensual signs can make ideal partners. Both are loyal and desire intimacy, but Scorpio's need for privacy may leave the Bull feeling stranded.

Gemini: This pairing is in for trouble: Gemini will find it difficult to meet Scorpio's stringent demands of a partner. Both signs may end up feeling betrayed.

Cancer: Two emotional partners can lead to a great deal of stress and drama. Scorpio can be fierce and will never back down; Cancer will have to be the conciliator for this relationship to work out.

Leo: One or both will have to relinquish some control for this match to work. But Scorpio will thrive in the warmth of Leo's love, and Leo will benefit from Scorpio's total devotion.

Virgo: Here is a couple capable of commitment. If Scorpio shows appreciation for the Virgin, and Virgo shares in Scorpio's passion, they can build a wonderful life together.

Libra: Scorpio would like to possess the lovely Libra, but Libra will never be happy in a gilded cage. Resentment and revenge could make this a dangerous liaison.

Scorpio: A successful combination, because Scorpios understand, respect, and, most importantly, trust each other. Social commitments and absorbing work will keep these two from too insular a life together.

Sagittarius: Scorpios can provide the depth, intuition, and healing that Sagittarians need, but frustration will develop if they try to possess these free spirits.

Capricorn: A potential for great passion and vigor exists when Capricorn's ambition and Scorpio's power are harnessed to love and a worthy goal.

Aquarius: The magnetic attraction between these two may be short-lived as Aquarians need more freedom in a relationship than Scorpios can tolerate.

Pisces: These two are on the same emotional wavelength. If Scorpio can give Pisces a little distance, and Pisces can be honest with Scorpio, this may turn into a lifetime of intimacy and romance.

*S*agittarius
(November 23–December 21)

Sagittarius is the sign of the Archer, the mysterious half-man, half-horse. Archers are adventurers and crusaders and their task is very simple: to follow their inner voices wherever they lead. Sagittarians are simultaneously teachers and students, always learning and always sharing what they have learned. Optimistic, loyal, enthusiastic, and generous to a fault, they are often pursued by others who admire their dedication. The truth is so important to them that they can often be blunt or tactless, but their intentions are never malicious. Sagittarians are notorious for their inability to commit and their free-spirited wandering. However, anything is possible with someone who understands their desire for greater knowledge—of themselves and the world.

Sagittarius &...

Aries: Sparks will fly between these two adventurers. A lifelong, passionate, and creative union is possible here though an unconventional lifestyle may be necessary.

Taurus: Sagittarius respects Taurus, and Taurus admires Sagittarius. However, the Bull's earthbound nature is sure to drag down the high-flying Archer.

Gemini: These two will-o'-the-wisps will hit it off with affection and stimulation to spare. Eventually, however, Gemini's busyness and Sagittarius's wanderlust will become troublesome.

Cancer: The Archer and the Crab are both givers by nature; this relationship may not strike a proper balance between giving and receiving.

Leo: A natural match between two warm, passionate, creative people capable of total devotion. Leo provides the support and Sagittarius provides the leadership.

Virgo: Though drawn together by shared ideals, the Archer may think Virgo's concerns too petty, and Virgo may find Sagittarius ridiculously impractical.

Libra: Libra cares most for the private life; Sagittarius for the greater good. Though these two can complement each other, conflict is inevitable.

Scorpio: Being challenged drives both Sagittarius and Scorpio—but it drives them in opposite directions. Sagittarius looks to the outside world for stimulation and Scorpio looks to the inner world.

Sagittarius: Two Archers can travel happily down the road of life together—but no one's left at home to pay the bills. Creative maneuvering will be necessary to make this impractical pairing pan out.

Capricorn: Two leaders going in opposite directions: Sagittarius off to save the world, and Capricorn up the ladder of success. Capricorn is much too bossy for Sagittarius, and the Goat will find the Archer's bluntness vulgar and offensive.

Aquarius: Friends, lovers, partners—this match has it all. Sagittarius and Aquarius are both brilliant crusaders dedicated to their convictions. Aquarius grounds Sagittarius, and Sagittarius will do anything for Aquarius.

Pisces: An alliance between the poet, Pisces, and the guru, Sagittarius, may be stimulating, but it won't last. Sagittarius will become impatient with Pisces' emotional upheavals and the sensitive Fish may feel under assault by the Archer's relentless truth telling.

Capricorn
(DECEMBER 22–JANUARY 20)

Capricorn, symbolized by the Goat, is the most committed of all the signs. They are mindful of time, duty, responsibility, and the awesome power of intense effort. The Goat's first commitment is the one to excellence: Capricorns need to excel at whatever they do. They absolutely must attain success, achieve real authority, and make their mark on the world. Self-respect and respect for others define the Goat, who places great value on tradition and family. To win their affections one must simply be true and consistent; Capricorns will naturally assume responsibility and authority. They enjoy giving advice, managing people, and solving problems. Unbridled ambition and a consuming career may not leave them much time for intimacy, but they are devoted to their family and friends.

Capricorn &...

Aries: Life together for these two leaders will be difficult. Capricorn is committed but Aries is absent; tension and misunderstandings will abound.

Taurus: A strong, loving bond based on shared values and friendship defines this pairing. Capricorn and Taurus will live up to their promises and build for the future.

Gemini: A sudden attraction often arises between these two. Gemini's lightness balances Capricorn's seriousness, and the Goat can provide the focus that Gemini lacks.

Cancer: A true marriage between committed, cooperative partners who share traditional values. Capricorn will protect and care for Cancer, and Cancer will nurture and support Capricorn.

Leo: If Capricorn is demonstrative with Leo, and Leo relinquishes a fair share of authority to the Goat, this can be a very prosperous alliance. Leo affirms; Capricorn commits.

Virgo: Two workaholics can forge a successful relationship as long as they remember to relax a little—and indulge each other.

Libra: These two signs complement each other as they strive together for the good life. Abundant affection and mutual respect highlight this match.

Scorpio: When they let down their formidable defenses, Capricorn and Scorpio can share a passionate and lasting love.

Sagittarius: The Goat can provide a safe refuge when Sagittarius becomes world-weary. In turn, the Archer's lightheartedness can be a soothing influence on the serious and hardworking Goat.

Capricorn: This team will conquer the world. Two Capricorns will set goals, work hard, and succeed. Shared roots are important here.

Aquarius: Diligence and leadership are Capricorn's contribution to this match; intelligence and insight are what Aquarius brings. If they share the same goals, a long-lasting commitment will be theirs.

Pisces: This is a devoted love-match. Capricorn is intrigued by Pisces' creative talents and spiritual quests, and Pisces' finds a stable home under the care and protection of the Goat.

Aquarius
(JANUARY 21–FEBRUARY 19)

Aquarius, the Water Bearer, is the most eccentric sign of the zodiac. Aquarians recognize their own uniqueness and view others as they view themselves, which makes them wonderful, supportive friends. The Water Bearers are savvy communicators whose ideas are frequently ahead of their time. They are devoted to their humanitarian pursuits and adamant about maintaining their own personal freedom. Although family is very important to the Water Bearers, the family of man is their real concern. And despite the fact that they are often self-sufficient loners, they can commit totally in a relationship based on true friendship, shared ideals, and individual freedoms.

Aquarius &...

Aries: These two will enjoy each other's independence. Aquarius sparks Aries' passion, and Aries encourages Aquarius to pursue brilliant ideas.

Taurus: Aquarius likes and respects Taurus, but the Bull's possessiveness will prove a burden to the liberty-loving Water Bearer.

Gemini: Wit and intelligence will light up a romance between Aquarius and Gemini, but it will take real commitment to make this relationship function on a day-to-day basis.

Cancer: This pair will find each other's eccentricities appealing—for a while. However, the sensitive and home-loving Crab will soon feel betrayed by the Water Bearer's insistence on autonomy.

Leo: Not a promising match. Leo is too demanding and touchy for Aquarius; Aquarius is too distant and eccentric for Leo.

Virgo: With an eye to the future and a headful of unproved ideas, Aquarius may find the Virgin's practical nature and focus on the here and now a bit less than stimulating.

Libra: Idealism and creativity will bring these two together easily. And love will last if they are affectionate with each other and don't let others lead them astray.

Scorpio: Though Aquarius and Scorpio tend to be loners, a certain magnetism draws them toward each other. Whether or not this attraction lasts depends upon their willingness to commit and to trust.

Sagittarius: Aquarius and Sagittarius are both inspired crusaders with their eyes on the future. Each, however, has a different agenda—making a romance impractical and practically impossible.

Capricorn: Strength of purpose binds Aquarius and Capricorn to their goals and it could bind them to each other—if they're willing to pursue their romance with the same focus that they pursue their other goals.

Aquarius: Friends forever. Though this union may lack somewhat in ardor, the depth of understanding and breadth of appreciation these two signs have for each other may outweigh other considerations.

Pisces: These two signs share talent and compassion. This can be a dedicated relationship, with room for individual expression and freedom.

Pisces
(FEBRUARY 20–MARCH 20)

Pisces, the last sign in the zodiac, is symbolized by two fish swimming in opposite directions. Pisceans are exceedingly sensitive, spiritual, intuitive, and creative. In touch with the muse, many Pisceans turn to poetry, painting, and music for expression; many others find themselves suited for teaching, preaching, and healing. Devotion is natural to them, so they seek a lifework, a belief system, or a spiritual practice to which they can give themselves. They are contemplative and need time alone. Though the Fish can frequently be withdrawn, moody, and unapproachable, it is also loving, giving, and responsive.

$\mathcal{P}$*isces&...*

Aries: A less than perfect union. Aries will often hurt Pisces' feelings and never know why. Pisces will find it difficult to be comfortable with the independent and rambunctious Ram.

Taurus: Pisces and Taurus share a warm affection for each other; both are sensual and creative. Taurus will probably end up managing this twosome, but despite its imbalance, this union is likely to last.

Gemini: Pisces and Gemini will never tire of each other's company, but romance is out of the question. Gemini is too flighty, and Pisces too needy, to sustain a serious relationship.

Cancer: These two are spiritually compatible, and capable of nurturing each other, but neither is strong enough to anchor the relationship on the physical plane.

Leo: Although these signs are both romantics, Leo's perpetual optimism and egocentric nature may prove too overpowering for the docile, introverted Pisces.

Virgo: These opposites should remain apart. Optimism and a broad perspective are vital, but missing in this pairing.

Libra: Pisces is charmed by Libra's graceful beauty, and Libra is thrilled by Pisces' romantic vision. Watch out though: Pisces may be too dreamy to meet Libra's demands, and Libra too cool to satisfy Pisces' sensitivity.

Scorpio: Intensity, sensuality, magnetism—all these will come into play in this potentially difficult match. Pisces must stake out real boundaries to protect its gentle nature from being overrun by the forceful Scorpio.

Sagittarius: These two love a cause but must instead focus on the relationship if it is to succeed. Both are prone to excesses and their life together could be more dramatic than either of them want.

Capricorn: Pisces will find the security Capricorn offers enticing, but will have to pay a price for it: relinquishing authority to the Goat. Once leadership is established, however, this match could go on forever.

Aquarius: This is an odd match, but these talented signs are capable of genuine love and support for each other. Though Pisces may find Aquarius a little too daring for comfort, life together can be rewarding.

Pisces: Two Pisceans can love and support each other forever. This could be a perfect match—especially if they share in a spiritual pursuit.